Apartheid

Published in 1986 by
Camden Press Ltd
43 Camden Passage, London N1 8EB, England

Text © Donald Woods
Illustrations © Mike Bostock
Designed by Terry Howe

Set in 11 on 12pt Palatino
by Character Typesetting, London EC1
and printed and bound by A. Wheaton & Co, Exeter

British Library Cataloguing in Publication Data

Woods, Donald
Apartheid: a graphic guide — (Graphic guides)
1, Blacks — South Africa — Segregation — History
2, South Africa — Race relations
I, Title II, Series
323,1′68   DT763
ISBN 0-948491-06-X

APARTHEID

A Graphic Guide

Text Donald Woods
Illustrations Mike Bostock

Camden Press

There is a country with

No Winters
No Hurricanes
No Tornadoes
No Blizzards
No Earthquakes

'No winters?'

Well, hardly. Most of the inhabitants have never seen snow.

'No earthquakes?'

Well, maybe every several hundred years.

'What is this — a desert?'

No, one of the most fertile countries on Earth. Intensively cultivated, it could feed the whole world.

'It must be heavily populated then.'

No, it is underpopulated. More than twice the size of Britain with barely half its population.

'There must be drawbacks. Is it ugly?'

On the contrary, it is one of the most beautiful countries in the world, with mountains, valleys, plains and great surf beaches . . .

'So it's got everything?'

Almost, including most of the world's Gold. Not to mention:
Diamonds
Platinum
Uranium
Vanadium
Manganese
and Chromium

'It sounds like Paradise!'

It was — before the Fall.

'You mean there's a snag?'

Er, yes . . . a big one. This Paradise is the most HATED country in the world . . .

....South Africa

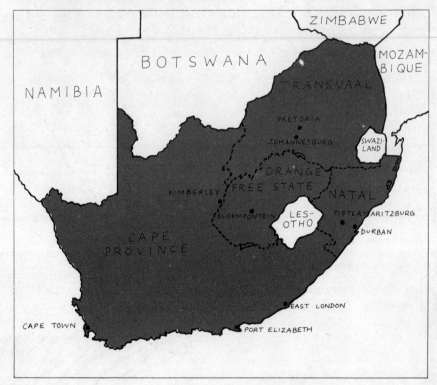

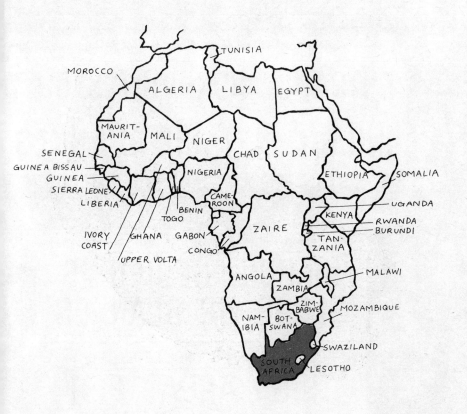

'The most hated country?'

Well, not the country — its Government, its political system. The system of APARTHEID:

ENTRANCE: NON-WHITES ONLY

INGANG: NET NIE-BLANKES

DIE AFDELINGSRAAD VAN DIE KAAP

HIERDIE GEBIED IS
SLEGS VIR BLANKES

OP LAS SEKRETARIS

THE DIVISIONAL COUNCIL OF THE CAPE

THIS AREA FOR
WHITES ONLY

BY ORDER•SECRETARY

WOMEN: NON-EUROPEANS ONLY

VROUE: NET NIE-BLANKES

WHITE PERSONS ONLY

THIS BEACH & THE AMENITIES THEREOF
HAVE BEEN RESERVED FOR WHITE
PERSONS ONLY   BY ORDER
PROVINCIAL SECRETARY

NET BLANKES

OP LAS
PROVINSIALE SEKRETARIS

BLANKES ALLEEN
WHITES ONLY

**PLAY   PARK   FOR
EUROPEAN   CHILDREN   ONLY
SPEELPARK   SLEGS**

VIR   BLANKE   KINDERS
OP LAS   BY ORDER
STADSKLERK   TOWN CLERK

Apartheid is a system of racial laws devised to preserve and promote white minority rule over the black majority. There are more than twenty three million black people and only five million whites.

'When did Apartheid start?'

Officially, in 1948.

'And unofficially?'

That's a long story. Let's begin at the beginning . . .

In the beginning was Africa — the continent about which there is more ignorance than any other.

People have strange notions about Africa, associating it mainly with images of jungle, poverty, harsh climate and political turmoil. They call it the Dark Continent — obscure, timeless and savage.

Jungle? There isn't much tropical rain forest in Africa, compared with South America and Asia. The fancy foliage in those old Tarzan movies is Californian, not African.

Poverty? Africa is the wealthiest of all the continents in minerals and natural resources, but this wealth has only recently begun to be developed for the benefit of Africans instead of for the Europeans who imposed their rule on Africa.

Harsh climate? No kinder climate for human habitation exists in the world than in most of Africa.

Political turmoil? There are 50 different countries in Africa, and their record of political stability this century — even including national liberation struggles — is better than Europe's, where many millions have died in civil and international wars.

The Dark Continent? Only to Europeans who thought Africa's history began with white explorers. The ancient civilisations of Africa were ahead of Europe's in science, technology and education.

Algebra began in Africa, as did most mathematics. Egyptians pioneered the geometry which Euclid and his Greek successors later developed.

The Sudanese evolved alphabetical script.

West Africans taught European traders how to fast-dye materials, the basis for the industrial manufacture of wool and cotton cloth from which much of Europe's wealth has grown.

The Moroccans had a university before most of Europe had elementary schools.

Africans had evolved techniques of mortarless building in stone as diverse as the pyramids in the north and the Zimbabwe citadel in the south. These structures remind us that they had sophisticated social systems before Europe's Middle Ages.

'So what happened? How did Africa come to be ruled by Europeans?'

First, Africa lost the cream of its youth through the slave trade. Young men and women were seized from their villages and transported to other countries, chiefly in the New World, to be sold as work-objects.

14

And then came the 'Scramble for Africa', as the London *Times* called it. During the 18th and 19th centuries, Africa was carved up for colonisation and control by the British, French, Portuguese, Germans, Belgians, Spanish and Dutch. Its territories became colonies, the spoils of Europe's interminable wars, treaties and commercial deals. In many cases whole new countries were created by the arbitrary drawing of lines on maps. Virtually every part of Africa was eventually in the possession of one or other European country.

But by the dawn of the 20th century the main 'owners' of Africa were Britain and France.

Britain controlled most of the north-east (Egypt, Sudan), east (Kenya, Uganda), west (Nigeria, Ghana), centre (Zambia, Malawi) and south (Zimbabwe and South Africa), with scattered bits along the way, such as Lesotho, Botswana and Swaziland.

France ruled most of north-west Africa (Algeria, Morocco), and much of the west (Senegal, Mali) — altogether more than 20 of modern Africa's 50 countries. It was to police its Saharan colonies that France formed the French Foreign Legion.

Lesser colonial owners were Portugal (Mozambique, Angola), Belgium (Zaire, Ruanda-Urundi), Spain (parts of Morocco and the Sahara), Germany (Namibia, Tanzania) and Italy (Ethiopia, Libya). The Germans and Italians lost their African colonies as a result of the world wars.

'What about the Dutch?'

Ah, the *Dutch!* Good question, because the Dutch first colonised South Africa in 1652, establishing a settlement at what is now Cape Town. At first their purpose was simply to supply meat, vegetables and water to the Dutch East India Company's fleets on their way to and from the Far East. Later, as it became an important trading station in its own right, settlers moved inland until the 'Cape Colony' was formed. In 1814, after the Napoleonic Wars, Britain 'acquired' the Colony from Holland, and in 1820 Britain sent in thousands of its own settlers.

The first Dutch settlers were soon joined by French Huguenots and by some German settlers, and together they evolved into a community called the Afrikaners (people of Africa), with their own language — Afrikaans. Since most worked the land they described themselves as *Boers*, which in Afrikaans means 'farmers'.

Afrikaans evolved from Dutch. As influence from Holland waned over 150 years, the colonists simplified their speech and dropped the more complicated rules of Dutch grammar. On the frontier there was no need for the drawing-room niceties of speech appropriate to Amsterdam, and in time Afrikaans became quite distinct from Dutch. Today, Afrikaans sounds more like modern Flemish. It is a vigorous language, with a thriving literature.

Afrikaans is spoken by about two thirds of South Africa's white population of five million.

The remaining third are mostly descendants of the British settlers who have arrived since 1820. But, there are other, smaller, English-speaking communities, such as Greeks, who gave up shipbuilding in the old country to become owners of many all-purpose shops in South Africa, and Jews who came from Eastern Europe, mostly Lithuania. But politically the Afrikaners are the dominant whites. They have ruled South Africa continuously since the British gave up control in 1910. In 1948 the Party most of them supported, the Afrikaner Nationalist Party, took power, introduced Apartheid and formed the administration still controlling South Africa in 1986 under President P. W. Botha.

'So it was the Afrikaner Nationalists who introduced Apartheid?'

Yes. *Apartheid* is an Afrikaans word meaning separate-ness. It is pronounced 'apart-hate'. In Afrikaans a *d* on the end of a word is usually pronounced as a 't', and *ei* has the sound of 'ay'.

Many things led to Apartheid; many fears, phobias, and fights. Although it began officially in 1948, Apartheid started unofficially as soon as the first Dutch settlers arrived in 1652. The country they came to settle was inhabited by various indigenous communities, and when the white settlers moved inland this meant the displacement of black people from their territory — a key element of Apartheid.

The biggest community was that of the Nguni — intelligent, physically strong people with ordered social and political structures. Partly indigenous and partly descended from waves of migrants who had come from Central and East Africa centuries before, they had long mined and smelted copper and iron, and had a vigorous pastoral and agricultural economy based mainly on cattle herds. They grew various crops — mainly corn and vegetables — and all land was owned communally, occupancy being decided by councils of elders on a tenancy basis. Farmers could keep and sell the crops they produced, but not barter or sell the land itself.

When the Nguni first encountered white settlers they were astonished at the white concept of individual ownership of land, likening it to the idea of owning 'the air we breathe, and the rain which falls.'

But goods were something else. Cattle, sheep and goats could be individually owned, as were spears, hoes and harrows. Such property was bartered on a large scale, the Nguni being noted traders throughout southern Africa. They were also noted warriors.

In recent centuries the Nguni in different areas of South Africa have become known by particular names: in Zululand as Zulus, in Swaziland as Swazis, in Matabeleland as Matabeles and further south as Xhosas.

> As with the lines on the colonial maps, the white officials couldn't always handle local nuances of pronunciation, so put arbitrary spellings to people and places. For example, the Nguni prefix *ama* refers collectively to people, so the Ndebele called themselves *ama-Ndebele*. The colonial clerks started writing this as Amadebele, then as Amatabele, then as Matabele. But linguistically and culturally, all these Zulu, Xhosa, Swazi and Ndebele 'tribes' were and remain Nguni, sharing common historical origins with people as far afield as Zimbabwe, Zambia, Malawi, Kenya, Tanzania and Uganda.

When whites first came to South Africa the Nguni were the majority black group in the country, and they still are. There were other black groups closely or distantly related in origin — the Sotho, Pedi, Shangani and others — but the Nguni were dominant in the north, east, centre and south of the country.

In the west, though, the predominant groups were nomadic hunters and gatherers, the Khoi and the San, who seldom planted crops as the Nguni did. Another difference was that they hunted with poisoned arrows, whereas the Nguni used spears. The San were fine artists, and their rock-paintings are to be found in many parts of the country.

The first recorded encounters between whites and blacks in South Africa took place more than a hundred years before the first white colonial settlers arrived from Holland. A group of Portuguese sailors, shipwrecked on the south-east coast in the fifteenth century, lived among the Nguni for several years before attracting the attention of a ship passing that remote coast. Their accounts, like the others who encountered the Nguni in the 15th and 16th centuries, emphasised the peaceable qualities of these people.

They noted that the Nguni were kind and hospitable, and gave them bread which they called *soncoa* (a Portuguese phonetic rendering of the Xhosa word for bread — *sonka*).

But they weren't to stay friendly.

When later generations of white settlers started encroaching on their territory the Zulu and Xhosa warriors of the 17th and 18th centuries resisted with such effect that their fame as fighters spread to Europe.

But the San and the Khoi were the first to experience permanent white settlement, when the Dutch established their

21

colonial foothold at the Cape in 1652. They called the San *Boesmanne* (Bushmen) and the Khoi *Hottentots*, a reference to the clicks in the Khoi language. Some of these distinctive clicks were later incorporated into the Xhosa language.

Both groups were increasingly driven inland when the Dutch expanded their settlement. They resisted this expansion but arrows were no match for muskets.

So Apartheid began with the dispossession of black people from their land — territorial Apartheid. But sexual Apartheid soon appeared as well when the settler leader, Jan Van Riebeeck, tried to stop his men having sexual relations with the Khoi and San women.

To this end, Van Riebeeck ordered the building of a wall around the settlements using a prickly type of thorn hedge called *Wag-'n-bietjie-bos* (the Wait-a-minute-bush). It was singularly ineffective as a first-strike deterrent, though, as the large numbers of 'mixed race' children born at the Cape soon proved.

Such children born of black and white parents were called 'Coloured' — a term which was to last for hundreds of years in South Africa. This was the beginning of the 'Coloured community', a group which has been augmented by many generations of inter-racial sex between blacks and whites, and whites and Malays brought to the Cape as slaves by the Dutch. The community has now grown to more than two million, many of whom are Muslims (the teachings of Islam having been brought in by the slaves from the Dutch colonies of the East Indies).

The 'Coloureds' were discriminated against from the beginning, but it was mild discrimination compared to what was to come in 1948 with the official launching of Apartheid.

The early, unofficial version allowed some lighter-skinned 'Coloureds' to be accepted as whites. One such 'Coloured' man, Simon Van Der Stel, even became a governor of the Cape Colony, and has the town regarded as the centre of Afrikaner culture, Stellenbosch, named after him. Yet more than 200 years later the Afrikaner Nationalists brought in laws making it illegal for 'Coloureds' to have civil rights, let alone to aspire to high office.

The racism of most Afrikaners was to increase the further inland they settled, especially on encountering stiffer resistance from the Nguni than they had from the San and Khoi.

And the Afrikaners acquired an added enemy when the British took over the Cape Colony in 1814. It was the start of what was to be a longstanding feud between the British and the Afrikaners; a feud which was to result, at the end of the 19th century, in the Boer war.

'How did the feud start?'

To begin with, the Afrikaners naturally resented the British coming in to rule them; they felt their language and culture was threatened. But their strongest objection was to the 'liberal' approach of the British to black people. The British, you see —

Allowed black people elementary civil rights

Gave them equal access to the courts

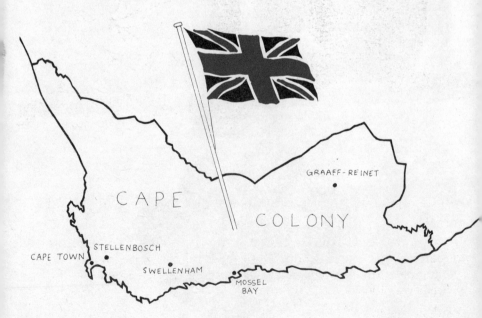

And worst of all from the Afrikaners' point of view, abolished slavery!

For many Afrikaners this was the last straw. Their farms depended on slave labour, and even those who agreed to emancipate their slaves felt the compensation offered by the British was too low.

And so began . . .

THE GREAT TREK

The remarkable mass-migration known as the Great Trek also had deeper motivations for the Afrikaners, based as it was on a mystical concept later to be central to the Apartheid system.

The Afrikaners had inherited from their Dutch and Huguenot forebears a narrow religious tradition based on their own interpretation of Calvinist teaching. It was puritanical, strict as to Sabbath observance, condemnatory of 'contact' dancing, drinking and 'frivolity', and it gave them a *mission* — to 'civilise' South Africa. They regarded themselves as the new Chosen People of the Old Testament, covenanted not only to inherit the new Promised Land of South Africa but also to keep themselves forever as a nation apart from others, distinctive in itself, with its own language. They saw themselves as a People with a Destiny.

From this it followed that it was part of their God-given mandate to remain separate in all ways from the 'heathens' of their new homeland, to permit no admixture of blood or culture through sexual laxity. As they saw it, God had created black people as different creatures, as distinct from them as all the separate species of fishes, birds and mammals of the Creation were from one another. And their 'divine law' required the active maintenance of such difference.

Initially this led to certain theological problems. While Calvin had found cause to celebrate the distinctions in the Creation, he had not been specific about races of human beings. (Indeed Calvinism laid stress on the inherent equality of individuals politically). Was it not the duty of Afrikaners to regard the indigenous 'savages' of South Africa as their fellow equals? Their brothers and sisters in Christ?

No Way!

This is how they argued their case:

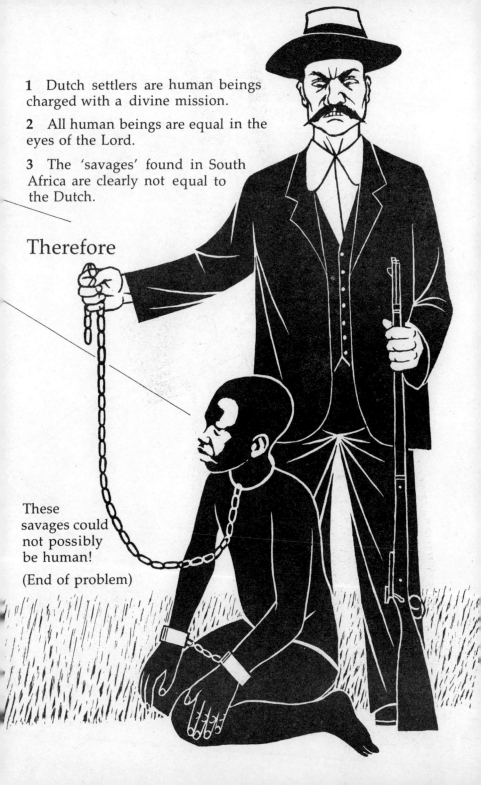

1 Dutch settlers are human beings charged with a divine mission.

2 All human beings are equal in the eyes of the Lord.

3 The 'savages' found in South Africa are clearly not equal to the Dutch.

Therefore

These savages could not possibly be human!

(End of problem)

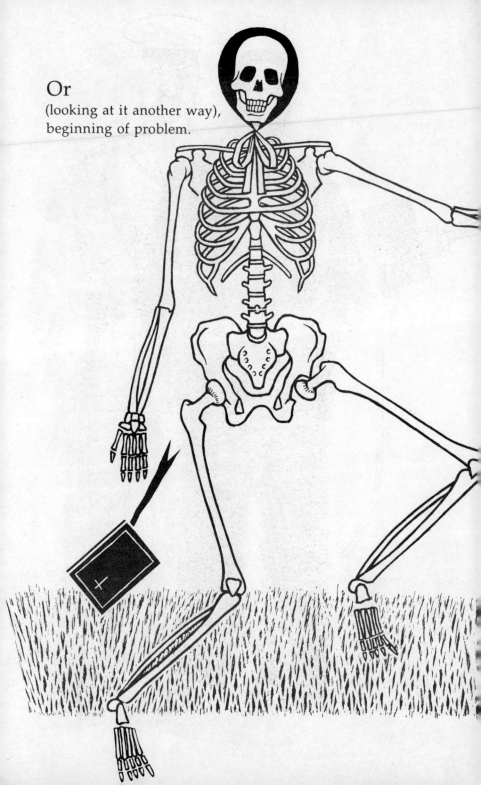

Or
(looking at it another way),
beginning of problem.

Other refinements were soon added to this basic 'theology'. The main one ran like this: According to the Old Testament, Noah had once partaken too liberally of the fruit of the vine. His son Ham, beholding his drunken father lying with his clothing in disarray, had laughed at him and mocked him, yea, verily unto ridicule. For this Jehovah had cursed Ham and punished him, saying that his descendants would forever after be hewers of wood and drawers of water.

To the early Dutch settlers with their own zany brand of Calvinism, the implications were clear. These 'savages' now confronting them in the new Promised Land were none other than these descendants of Ham. Servants. Slaves. Their divinely ordained task was obviously to hew wood and draw water for the settlers!

'Good theology there, Jan.'

'Thanks, Piet, I kinda like it myself.'

So, in abolishing slavery and in treating these savages almost as human beings, the hated British were not only getting up the noses of the Afrikaner Boers, they were getting up God's nose as well. They were ruining the divine plan to keep the Boers supplied with cheap Hamitic servants.

So the Promised Land must be elsewhere, further north, where the Afrikaners could establish their own Boer republics with their own Hamitic servants, away from the hated British and answerable only to Jehovah himself.

Hence . . .

The Great Trek

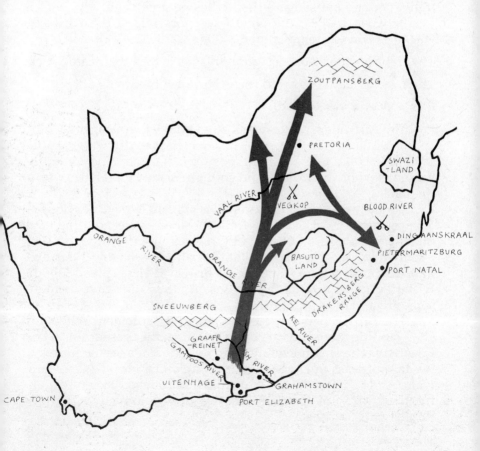

Afrikaners were the new Chosen People wandering through the wilderness, like the Jews of the Old Testament escaping from bondage to the new Canaan.

The Afrikaners trekked and trekked in search of the new Promised Land, and as they trekked, small groups of them hived off to begin their own settlements. Of course, as they trekked and settled further into the hinterland they encountered increasingly angry Nguni warriors who didn't want their grazing land trekked over and settled on by these intruders.

This time the Nguni response to such intrusion wasn't bread, but the spear . . . But the Afrikaners didn't take the hint, and pushed on further into the interior. Fights began to break out, and fights became battles, and the battles became wars.

Between battles, the Nguni warriors raided the Afrikaner waggon-trains to remove the trekkers' cattle.

The trekkers attacked the Nguni villages to take their cattle back.

Then each side would raid the other for more than cattle.

It was now a blood feud!

The Afrikaners under attack would draw their waggons into a defensive circle — a 'laager' — into which they drove their cattle. The men would take up firing positions between and under the waggons while the women and children loaded their rifles within the circle.

Today the Afrikaner Nationalists are said to have developed a 'laager mentality' as a legacy from those times, responding to all external problems and threats by retreating within themselves. Meanwhile, on other fronts, the British were having their own battles against Nguni warriors. As British settlers spread into the Eastern Cape and Natal the Xhosas and the Zulus gave them the same treatment.

The British had started their biggest settlement scheme in 1820, landing thousands of young Britons at the present site of Port Elizabeth. They hadn't volunteered for sheer love of adventure but because of mass unemployment in England after the Napoleonic wars. And besides, the government had promised each settler one hundred acres of farmland in the new colony, free farming implements and seed.

It took them months to sail to this new world, and the part where they landed reminded them of home. It was as green as Hampshire, with rolling Downs like Sussex, and when they swarmed ashore they founded towns with names like Bathurst in the district of Albany, which soon sprouted a pub called the 'Pig and Whistle'. But there the resemblance to England ended. They soon discovered that one hundred acres in South Africa yielded less than five acres in England: the soil didn't suit their seed and few of the promised farming implements were ever supplied.

Being stoic Anglo-Saxons they shrugged their shoulders and settled down anyway, many of them in the vicinity of Grahamstown. Most reverted to their earlier trades as blacksmiths, coopers, carpenters and builders. And there in the limitless veld, with all the space in the world, they built tiny houses like the ones they had left behind in England, with cramped little gardens and picket fences.

Although they were neither particularly idealistic nor parti-

cularly imaginative, they nevertheless had the habits of free men, and out of habit they founded the colony's first free press. And though they weren't very liberal, again out of habit they founded the colony's first liberal university.

It dawned on them only after some time that their real purpose in the eyes of the colonial government was not to grow rich on agriculture in this new world, but to be the buffer between the Afrikaners and the Xhosas in their territorial war of attrition — to be the filling in the frontier sandwich.

So when the Afrikaners trekked north away from this troublesome zone filled with Britishers, freed slaves and defiant Xhosas, the British troops and settlers bore the brunt of the territorial wars in the Eastern Cape, as they were also to do in Natal against the Zulus. The British troops found the Nguni to be among the fiercest fighters encountered anywhere in the scattered lands of the Empire. Skirmishes and tense truces regularly alternated with full-scale wars.

This went on for years before the British finally broke Zulu military power in Natal at the battle of Ulundi (1879), after heavy British losses in the battles of Isandhlwana and Rorke's Drift.

The same was true down in the Cape, where the Xhosas fought no fewer than nine wars before they were defeated — and even then it was through self-inflicted injury, the tragedy of The Great Cattle Killing. In 1856 it was said that a young girl named Nongqause had prophesied that if the Xhosas slaughtered all their cattle warriors would rise up in their place to drive away the white invaders. A huge massacre of cattle occurred all over the Eastern Cape. In the famine which followed thousands of Xhosas starved to death, giving the British the victory they'd been unable to win through physical force.

To this day some Xhosa historians believe that Nongqause had been in the pay of a British official, which has led some Xhosas to share at least one common emotion with Afrikaner Nationalists ever since — a deep distrust of the British.

So with Nguni power broken in the east and south by the British and in the north and central areas by the Afrikaners, the Cape Colony and Natal became self-governing British states while Transvaal and Orange Free State became independent Boer republics.

'What of the indigenous people in these four white-ruled states?'

In the two Boer republics there was no doubt about black rights. They didn't have any. (Black people not being entirely human, remember?)

In the two British colonies some rights were conceded, particularly in the Cape Province where black people could gain the vote by proving they could read and write, by owning property or by earning a salary of a fixed amount. The 'Coloureds' were given voting rights without such qualification.

In 1860 the British added a fourth racial community to South Africa when they introduced indentured Indian labour into the Natal sugar plantations. This Indian community has now grown to almost a million.

For a time the two British states co-existed fairly amicably with the two republics. But then diamonds were discovered at Kimberley in the Orange Free State and gold was discovered in the Transvaal.

The response of the British to the first find was instant — they simply lopped off the corner of the Orange Free State which contained Kimberley and annexed it to the Cape Province.

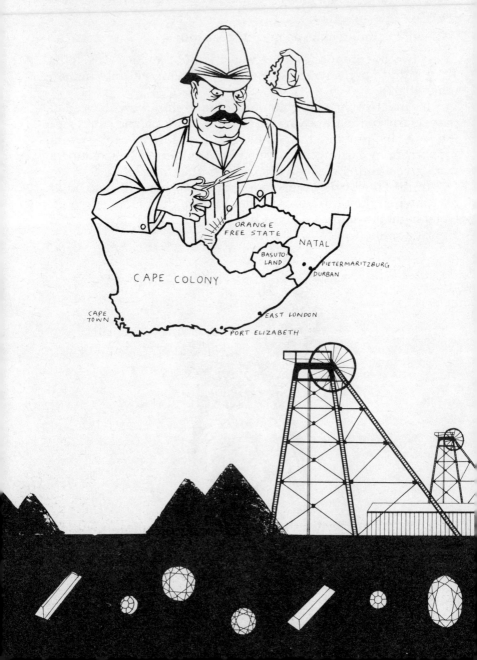

The Gold Question was a bit more complicated because the gold discovery wasn't on a snippable corner of the Transvaal — it was deep inside its borders.

Besides, the Transvaal had a very tough President: Paul Kruger.

Coarse and barely literate, Kruger was shrewd and ornery, but most of all he was tough. Before the age of 15 he had killed a lion and cut off his own thumb when it became infected. And when a water-buffalo had attacked him on a river bank, he had wrestled it to death by holding its nostrils under the water until it drowned . . . Before he was 40, Kruger had been elected President of the Transvaal Republic.

In Kruger's Transvaal Republic only Afrikaners or whites of long residence were recognised as citizens while all non-Afrikaners were regarded as Uitlanders (foreigners). So he didn't like it one bit when the discovery of gold brought people flocking in from all over the world. He particularly didn't like it that most of them were British.

Yet he needed the gold because his country was broke, so he had no choice but to use the technology and expertise of the Uitlanders. But he watched with increasing distaste as Johannesburg, City of Gold, mushroomed into a metropolis with saloons, dance-halls, loose women and — horrors — 'contact dancing'.

Uncompromising in his strict brand of Dutch Reformed Church Calvinism, Kruger proclaimed Johannesburg the Sodom and Gomorrah of the Promised Land, and would only visit it on ceremonial occasions. Addressing a civic audience there in his official capacity, he once began a speech: 'Citizens, Strangers, Scoundrels and Thieves . . .' And at the official inauguration of a new synagogue, he declared it open: 'In the name of Our Lord Jesus Christ.'

As goldmining prospered, the Uitlanders quickly outnumbered the Transvaal Afrikaners themselves.

They demanded the vote.

Kruger said no.

The argument raged for years. The Uitlanders could see the potential of a well-run Transvaal, which under Kruger they saw as inefficient, corrupt and resistant to modernisation. For his part Kruger saw the aliens as a threat to the way of life of the Afrikaners in their Promised Land; in his scenario they were now the Philistines.

42

And others took a hand in the quarrel. Down in Cape Town, the Prime Minister of Cape Colony turned a covetous eye on Kruger's Transvaal gold.

And he knew something about mining, this Prime Minister. He was Cecil Rhodes, diamond king of the world and controller of the Kimberley diamond cartel.

Rhodes had no doubts that the British should and would eventually control the whole world — in its own best interest, of course, which is why he set up his Rhodes Scholarships to produce the world's future rulers. More immediately, he believed that all of Africa, from 'Cape to Cairo', should be British-owned, and to that end he helped 'annexe' what became known as Northern and Southern Rhodesia to the British Empire. (On his death bed Rhodes said anxiously: 'They don't . . . change the names of countries, do they?' But they do. Northern Rhodesia later became Zambia and Southern Rhodesia is now called Zimbabwe.)

But here was a chunk of territory blocking the link between his Cape Colony and the rest of British Africa — the Transvaal Republic. And it had all that gold.

Using the fact that most of the Uitlanders demanding the vote in the Transvaal were British, Rhodes and the colonial authorities in London began a campaign of threats against Kruger, including invasion 'to protect the rights of the Uitlanders'. In 1899, that sparked off . . .

The Boer War

Although it was basically a war between whites, the Boer war profoundly shaped future white attitudes to blacks, and some results of the war led directly to Apartheid.

The Boer war lasted more than two years. At first the Transvaal, allied with the Orange Free State, fought against troops from the Cape, Natal and Britain itself. But by the end of the war the two Boer republics were up against the entire British Empire, with reinforcements arriving from Canada, Australia and New Zealand.

It was a strange, horrible war; in some ways the last of the 'gentlemanly' wars and the first of the 'total' wars.

It started out with rules, though. When the Boers were besieging Ladysmith, Mafeking and Kimberley, they wouldn't shell on Sundays, though some of them fired a few disapproving shots at Mafeking when they saw the British soldiers making use of the Sabbath truce to play cricket. Such sinful behaviour shocked the Boers. And on Christmas Day in Mafeking the Boers fired a dud shell into the British camp. It contained a Christmas pudding and the message: 'Compliments of the Season'.

All very friendly. Very civilised.

At first. Then things started getting nasty.

Initially this arose through misunderstandings. For example, to the British the worst crime in war was to fight under false colours — to sneak up on your opponent wearing his uniform. And this is what the Boers did. But their real reason was not fundamentally tactical. With their coats in tatters, many Boers were short of clothing in the field and suffered terribly from cold at night, they had no choice but to take the tunics from the British dead.

Another source of enmity arose when epidemics of dysentery raged through Boer communities under British occupation. The British medics prescribed salts to replace lost body fluids (which was a reasonable thing to do at the time). But when children died in spite of such treatment the Boers, whose knowledge of modern medicine was minimal, thought the salts must be ground glass, and the belief spread that the British were murdering them.

But the most lasting bitterness resulted from the British policy of putting Afrikaner families and their black servants into concentration camps.

'Concentration camps?'

That's what they were called! The British invented them. The idea was to concentrate the civilian population in tent camps, and burn their homes and crops to stop the Afrikaner guerillas using them as supply bases. They were Lord Kitchener's bright idea. Total war, as in two later world wars. And when enteric fever and other diseases swept through these insanitary camps, it resulted in the death of more than 35,000 whites and 50,000 blacks.

The Boer War added to the hatred between whites and blacks. Some Boer leaders, like General Hertzog, summarily executed black people pressed into service on the British side. Among the worst atrocities were several massacres by Boers of whole black villages for no military reason at all. War intensified the already deep anti-black prejudice of most Afrikaners (though as we shall see later, two exceptions were the leading young Boer generals, Jan Smuts and Louis Botha).

But the war brought out the worst in both sides. Some British leaders, later to be regarded as heroes, had a bad record as well. Lord Baden-Powell, for example, founder of the Boy Scout movement, was honoured for leading Mafeking throughout its siege. But what is generally not mentioned is that he had brought the garrison and the white community through near-starvation only by cutting down on the rations of the blacks to feed the whites.

'Was no country in the world sympathetic to the Boers?'

Several were, in principle, but the only country that openly helped them with guns and supplies was Germany. Which made Queen Victoria very angry with her nephew, the Kaiser.

'So the Boers were grateful to the Germans?'

Yes, and this had something important to do with the bringing in of Apartheid 46 years later.

'But how?'

We'll come to that later. Inevitably the Boers lost to greater numbers. When this war ended in 1902, they were a shattered nation. They had lost the cream of their young men, women and children, their farms, homes, possessions and crops. But most of all they had lost their Promised Land.

They were now ruled by the hated British.

BOTHA

SMUTS

Before the end of the war Kruger had fled into exile to die in Switzerland, and his demoralised followers turned for leadership to the two young heroes of the war — Louis Botha and Jan Smuts.

In the politics of reconciliation with the British Botha and Smuts were both to provide statesmanship of a high order, although like most whites of their time they were blind to the issue of rights for black people.

GANDHI

At this period of the Boer War and its immediate aftermath there were other interesting personalities on the South African scene who were later to come to international prominence.

One was Mahatma Gandhi, who served in a medical unit on the British side during the war. He had come to South Africa to defend the rights of Indians but had gone on to campaign for democratic freedoms for all South Africans, developing tactics of passive resistance which were to prove so successful against British rule when he returned to India in 1914.

Another was Winston Churchill. In the heat of battle Churchill had shed his war correspondent status and taken up arms. He was captured, and by escaping from a Pretoria prison was catapulted to fame and Parliament in Britain.

A third was Rudyard Kipling, who wrote extensively about the war and stayed on for a time to work as a journalist in postwar South Africa.

And of course there was Lord Kitchener. His idea of burning the homes of his enemies and herding their families into concentration camps resulted in almost as many deaths through disease as his generalship was later to cause on Europe's battlefields in World War I.

HERTZOG

With Kruger in exile and Rhodes dead, two new arch-opposites emerged.

One was Britain's post-war administrator in South Africa, Lord Milner. He added to the sufferings of the defeated Boers by trying to stamp out their Afrikaans language and identity. Schoolchildren heard speaking Afrikaans instead of English had insulting signs hung about their necks.

The other was General Hertzog, the man who had summarily executed blacks he regarded as serving the British cause. Hertzog opposed the conciliatory policies of Botha and Smuts and started laying the foundations of the Afrikaner Nationalist Party that would one day introduce Apartheid.

At first, Hertzog's attempts to rekindle Afrikaner nationalism gained little or no support. The Afrikaners were sick of war and too demoralised to practise his politics of confrontation with the victorious British. And besides, Hertzog couldn't match the heroic image of Smuts and Botha. These two won overwhelming support from Afrikaners for their policy of peaceful co-operation with the British-descended South Africans for a united (white) South Africa.

Smuts and Botha had a shrewd understanding of the British character, and both realised that if they played their cards right they could win back from the British in peace what they had lost in war. And more . . .

Smuts had genius. Although he spoke no English until he was in his teens, he won a scholarship to Cambridge University (of which, one day, he would become Chancellor) and graduated with honours. On his return to the Transvaal and still in his twenties, he was appointed Attorney-General of the Republic. When the Boer War broke out he swiftly rose to the rank of General. His men worshipped him and he commanded the most successful guerilla unit of the war.

In the following years Smuts became Prime Minister of South Africa and member of the Imperial War Cabinet in World War One. He coined the phrase 'Commonwealth of Nations', and after World War Two he drafted the preamble to the Charter of the United Nations. Yet he continued his intellectual work too (he carried Greek and Latin classics in his saddlebags throughout the Boer war). He was a philosopher who developed a theory of evolutionary holism, a botanist who classified more species of grasses on Table Mountain alone than exist throughout the British Isles, and a writer and orator of world renown.

Louis Botha was even more charismatic — his senior officers used to weep if he so much as lost a friendly game of chess. But he recognised the genius of Smuts, and together they campaigned for independence for a united (white) South Africa.

The British were charmed by these two, seeing them as former foes turned loyal allies. And when a Liberal government came to power in London it granted independence to the new Union of South Africa. Natal and Cape Province were joined to the Transvaal and the Orange Free State with Botha as Prime Minister and Smuts as his deputy. The new Union was given the status of a Dominion under the Crown, like Australia and Canada.

Black people in South Africa campaigned ceaselessly against this 'independence', pointing out to the British that it denied rights to the majority of South Africa's population.

Several groups even travelled to London to make their objections known to the British government. One of the ablest of the new black politicians was Sol Plaatje, who led two of these delegations with a skill that impressed Lloyd George. Speakers addressed meetings all over Britain to try to influence public opinion away from the adulation of Smuts and Botha but it was still not enough to reverse British policy.

By granting independence to the Union of South Africa on these terms, the first cornerstone of Apartheid was laid: the British had delivered the black majority in the country into the hands of the white minority. Once this had happened, the structure of Apartheid began to take shape.

Although Botha and Smuts were comparative moderates in their attitude to black people, it was made clear by the increasing numbers of Hertzogites that the price of their support would be measures to further limit black rights. The resulting compromise was the Native Land Act, the first of many increasingly restrictive property laws. Already without voting rights in most of the country, black people were now barred from owning land in three quarters of the national territory. A further move was the setting aside for them of reservations known as the Native Territories.

A.N.C. 1912

The response of black people was to form the African National Congress through which they could campaign for equal rights. Moderate in style and led by intellectuals, the ANC soon became the premier black movement of South Africa. The ANC relied on reasoned petitions and delegations to the white government to object to racial legislation. Their efforts were unsuccessful, and the first racial laws were soon passed in the new South African Parliament.

In fact, the Native Land Act did nothing to placate Hertzog. In 1914, he began to rally support for his new Afrikaner Nationalist Party. Hertzog's argument was simple. The facts, he said, were obvious; the solution was self evident:

Had the Afrikaners not been crushed in war by the perfidious British?

Was not their 'independence' purely nominal, since they were under the British Crown?

Were Botha and Smuts not too co-operative with the British and too soft on the blacks?

Reunited under the new party, Afrikaners would easily outnumber the English-speaking (white) South Africans, so they could restore their Afrikaans language and culture to paramountcy and seize back power in their own country.

His call had a strong appeal to some Afrikaners, but Botha and Smuts still had many admirers and Hertzog probably wouldn't have got much further if two things hadn't occurred. One was World War I, in which Britain tested the friendship of Botha and Smuts and received their uncompromising support. The other was the formation of the Afrikaner Broederbond.

Botha and Smuts had gained control of South Africa from the British in 1910 on the understanding that South Africa would be a loyal Dominion of the British Empire in peace and in war. There was little problem about this in peacetime, because the resentful Afrikaners were never called on to do anything for the hated British. But when World War I broke out in 1914 and the British asked South Africa to help, there was uproar. Not only were Afrikaners being asked to side with the British, but they would be fighting against Germans, their only friends during the Boer War.

Nevertheless, Botha and Smuts honoured their pledge. But although they announced that only volunteers would be asked to fight, rebellion broke out among Hertzog supporters in the army. Botha and Smuts put it down firmly with some loss of life. They then rode off to fight a war on behalf of the British: Botha to lead the campaign in German South West Africa, and Smuts the one in German East Africa (probably history's only example of a Prime Minister and his deputy taking the field as active military commanders).

Botha defeated the German forces at Windhoek to take control of the large country which was later to be known as Namibia. The Germans had colonised the area during Europe's Scramble for Africa, putting down the rebellions of the indigenous people, the Herero, so ruthlessly that they were practically wiped out. They went on to consolidate their rule under a governor named Goering, whose son Hermann was to head the air forces of Hitler's Third Reich.

Meanwhile, over in German East Africa (later Tanzania) Smuts had equal success.

After the war, and in gratitude for services to the Allied cause, South Africa was given control of South West Africa by mandate of the League of Nations. But there was a proviso. Along with such control went the obligation to prepare the territory for self-rule which was to be followed swiftly by complete independence.

Today, after nearly 70 years, South Africa has yet to get around to the first task, much less to the second.

For helping the British, and especially for fighting against the Germans, Smuts and Botha lost even more support among Afrikaners. Hertzog's movement began to thrive.

Hertzog was not the only figure able to make political capital out of the war. So did a young man named Henning Klopper, who founded a secret society based on ritual oath-taking, the Afrikaner Broederbond (Afrikaner Brotherhood). The Broederbond had clear aims:

- To restore South Africa to Afrikaner Nationalist control (through the Hertzog party)

- To infiltrate Afrikaner Nationalists into key positions of influence politically, administratively and culturally.

- To promote strict laws of racial segregation (later to be called Apartheid laws).

- To place 12,000 members in influential positions in South African society, especially in the civil service, and to be the thinktank and power source for all racial legislation once the Afrikaner Nationalists won control.

Henning Klopper was also responsible for an extraordinary theatrical event which further boosted the surge towards Apartheid: a symbolic re-enactment of the Great Trek which rekindled fires of Boer feeling long dormant in the hearts of many Afrikaners.

In the mid '30s, Klopper organised hundreds of waggons from many parts of the country to converge on a site near Pretoria where the foundation stone was to be laid of a giant Voortrekker monument. Participants then made a pledge to reunite Afrikaners to form a new Boer Republic, this time covering all South Africa, where the interests of Afrikaners would be paramount and where black people would be kept in subjection.

Hertzog's Afrikaner Nationalist Party, later to equate anti-racist campaigns with 'communist agitation' and to make the teaching of communism a statutory crime, was one of the first political parties in the world to hail the Bolshevik takeover in Russia. It described the revolution as 'wonderful news — a great blow to the tyranny of capitalism and imperialism.' By the time Nazi Germany repudiated its own pact with Stalin by attacking the Soviet Union, the Afrikaner Nationalist party too had decided finally that communism was evil, decadent and immoral.

Between the two world wars the influence of Botha and Smuts began to wane as Hertzog's Afrikaner Nationalist Party, aided by Klopper's Broederbond, won increasing support among Afrikaners. (Indeed, for some years it was only the support of the English-speaking whites which kept the Botha-Smuts party in power.)

Then Louis Botha died. When World War 2 began Smuts again responded loyally to the British request for support, further alienating many Afrikaners.

Again South Africa's military contribution to the Allied cause had to be purely voluntary, because of the heated feelings on the issue in the Afrikaner community. Yet even so, Smuts still had a sufficiently large following to put into the field the biggest volunteer army among the Allies. In response, Afrikaner Nationalists formed paramilitary groups such as the Ossewa-Brandwag (Ox-waggon Guards), Die Gryshemde (The Greyshirts) and Die Nuwe Orde (The New Order) to beat up men in uniform and to sabotage bridges and military barracks.

Parallel with this upsurge in Afrikaner Nationalism was a fast-growing admiration for Germany's Nazi ideology. Initially based on well-remembered German support during the Boer War and on Hitler's anti-British stance, this admiration was increased by the appeal of his master-race theories which accorded well with their own belief in white superiority.

A further bond between the Afrikaner Nationalists and the Nazis in Germany was forged by a zealot named Hendrik Frensch Verwoerd.

How often zealous nationalist leaders have come from places other than the countries they idealise!

Napoleon was born in Corsica, not in France

Hitler was born in Austria, not in Germany

Stalin was born in Georgia, not in Russia

De Valera was born in America, not in Ireland

Verwoerd was born in Holland, not South Africa.

He was to prove a deadly immigrant.

Verwoerd had been brought to South Africa as a youth by his parents, then sent for his postgraduate education to Germany where his stay coincided with the rise of the Nazis. Verwoerd admired Hitler and worked to accord the Hitlerian doctrine of racial purity with the Afrikaner Nationalist variety to be called Apartheid. On his return to South Africa, Verwoerd was to play a prominent role in the Afrikaner Nationalist Party and to become known as the Grand Architect of Apartheid.

Although Hitler's Afrikaner Nationalist counterparts chiefly aimed their hostility against black people, they had a strong streak of anti-Semitism as well. South Africa had a substantial community of Jews mostly from central and eastern Europe. They had prospered as immigrants and contributed significantly to the development of mining, commerce and industry in South Africa. Many Afrikaners, still predominantly agricultural in outlook, resented their success, and the Afrikaner Nationalist Party press contained endless diatribes against 'British-Jewish Capitalism', inventing a cartoon character called Hoggenheimer who symbolised their idea of greed and exploitation. Heavily influenced by Nazi publications, the Afrikaner Nationalists fiercely opposed the acceptance by Smuts of Jewish refugees into South Africa.

Hertzog was ultimately thrown out of the party he had founded. The younger firebrands of Afrikaner Nationalism had decided that he was . . . too moderate!

Among the zealots who rejected him were several who would one day be immensely powerful figures in the South African government. Not just Verwoerd but

Dr. Daniel Malan	(future Prime Minister)
Mr Eric Louw	(future Foreign Minister)
Charles Swart	(future State President)
Johannes Strydom	(future Prime Minister)

. . . and a young firebrand even they were nervous of — Balthazar Johannes Vorster. Vorster had been a serving 'General' in the paramilitary underground, the Ossewa-Brandwag.

During World War 2 an understanding was reached between the leadership of the most militant wing of the Afrikaner Nationalist Party and the Nazi leadership in Berlin. A German victory in the war would lead to the institution of an Afrikaner Nationalist Republic in South Africa which would follow identical policies against Jews and black people according to their mutually held theory of Aryan race purity.

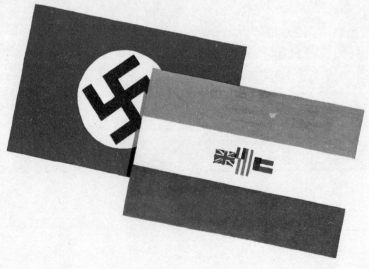

But the Allied victory frustrated these designs, and the militant Afrikaner Nationalists had to abandon the hope of a Promised Land restored by courtesy of the Third Reich. (Though the man the Germans had chosen as their Gauleiter in South Africa, Nico Diederichs, later became State President.)

But as the general election of 1948 drew near luck came to their aid and launched them into power.

One factor was the complacency of Jan Smuts. His party canvassers reported an upsurge in support for the Afrikaner Nationalist Party and begged him to restructure the chiefly rural voting districts in which the Afrikaner Nationalists were being given a 15% advantage in seats. He refused, saying this had never been necessary before and that 'his people' — Afrikaners as a whole — would not abandon him now.

Another was the degree to which Smuts was out of touch with domestic politics. On the world stage throughout the war, and now playing a leading role in the formation of the United Nations, he didn't realise the extent to which many Afrikaners resented his international prominence. They believed he was putting others' interests above their own.

A further issue was the bitterness of returned soldiers, many of whom had been prisoners of war for years. A particular grievance was that Smuts had still not delivered housing he had promised them as a reward. Most of these would not normally have voted for the Afrikaner Nationalists, but now did so in the twin belief that (a) the Afrikaner Nationalists could never win the election and (b) a bigger vote for them would be a rebuke for the Smuts government.

But the biggest boost to the vote for the Afrikaner Nationalists was the formulation of the policy known as . . .

Apartheid.

Apartheid was a new word, coined for the 1948 election campaign as a short way of referring to a whole package of legislation the Afrikaner Nationalists promised would be introduced if they came to power. It meant apartness — separateness — a promise to promote white privilege, remove all civil rights from blacks, and segregate all of South Africa's public amenities. The Afrikaner Republic would be re-established, bigger than before. The blacks would be put in their place. And . . . most of all . . . white purity would be preserved and white rule entrenched.

The Afrikaner Nationalists, under the leadership of Dr Daniel Malan, knew they would poll well, but not even they expected to win. But Apartheid served them well, and the Promised Land was regained. When the final result was announced, one old Afrikaner Nationalist Party worker stood with tears streaming down his face and declared: 'Even the trees look different!'.

The nightmare of Apartheid was about to be made real.

Malan was to be succeeded by Johannes Strydom (who changed the spelling of his name to Strijdom because it was more 'Boerlike'), Hendrik Verwoerd (the architect of Apartheid), Balthazar Vorster (former Ossewa-Brandwag 'General' who was imprisoned by Smuts during World War Two for subversive activities) and Pieter Botha, who was to be the last Prime Minister of the Apartheid Era.

Dr Daniel Malan

Dr. Daniel Francois Malan, who led the Afrikaner Nationalist
Party to victory on the promise of introducing Apartheid, was to
keep his word with a grim determination. A dour minister of the
Dutch Reformed Church, Malan was easily shocked. When driven
past the statue of the Manikin Pis on a state visit to Belgium he
turned away with his hands in front of his eyes, saying: 'Sinful
world! Sinful world!'
He was not only profoundly ignorant of the way of life and the
aspirations of his country's black people, but also that of his
fellow-whites of British descent. While being introduced to the
South African cricket team on the eve of their departure for a tour
of England, he said to Dudley Nourse, the team's captain, 'I hope
you enjoy your visit to South Africa.'

All of these promoted the Apartheid system in their various ways and styles, but Malan was the first, and he drew heavily on the legislative package of laws designed by Hendrik Verwoerd to lay the foundation stones of statutory Apartheid.

First, however, the Afrikaner Nationalists had to consolidate their grip on power. They started with a majority of only 5 seats in the 174 seat Parliament, though they increased this majority to 11 through victories in tiny 3000-vote constituencies in South West Africa (Namibia) controlled by the Party.

Then they:

Purged the military and civil service, replacing non-Afrikaner Nationalists with Broederbond-approved Party activists.

Removed the right of 'coloureds' in Cape Province to vote, and passed laws reserving the franchise to whites only.

Redrew the boundaries of all constituencies, ensuring that they could never be voted out of power.

Passed laws strictly limiting rights of opposition, freedom of expression and assembly.

Turned over the state broadcasting and education systems to Party nominees approved by the Broederbond.

What remained of parliamentary democracy, even for whites, was reshaped to suit the Afrikaner Nationalist Party. When Opposition senators voted to block the removal of the 'coloured' vote on the grounds that the British-granted constitution of 1910 required a two-thirds vote of both Houses of Parliament, the Afrikaner Nationalists simply passed a law empowering them to create extra senators, then nominated enough extra senators to make up the numbers needed for the two-thirds majority.

Of course there had never been real parliamentary democracy in South Africa — only some forms of it pertaining to whites and to 'coloureds' in the Cape — but even the vestiges were now to be transformed.

Instead of legislation emanating from the expressed wishes of voters at grassroots level, travelling upward through resolutions at party congresses as in many democratic countries, the process was now reversed. Policy decisions were henceforth made by the Governing Council of the Broederbond, transmitted to the Cabinet and passed downward to be echoed in a 'parliamentary vote' with only token debate from the party representatives. Parliament became a rubber stamp for the demands of the Broederbond, and it was to stay that way throughout the long administration of the Afrikaner Nationalist Party.

Now they were ready to introduce Apartheid.

Some of the groundwork had already been done. There were racist customs in the country — for example by tacit agreement blacks did not go to certain places — and there were also racist laws. But they weren't severe enough for the Afrikaner Nationalists. Customs and laws had to be systematically codified as part of a comprehensive package of strict statutory segregation.

The laws already existing contained certain prohibitions against inter-racial marriage, and there was a curfew and pass law system limiting free movement of black people, as well as the land acts setting up the reservations. But these were now to be revised, sharpened up, and made comprehensive. Apartheid was to mean total segregation of the races at every level of existence throughout the country, and applied to every citizen; it was ultimately to remove even the citizenship of black people.

Having consolidated power, the Afrikaner Nationalists unfolded the legislative package of Apartheid laws according to the Verwoerd formula.

The keystone of Apartheid was the reservation of the franchise in white, and particularly in Afrikaner Nationalist, hands.

To police this and make sure no borderline cases slipped through, the **RACE CLASSIFICATION ACT** was passed, classifying every South African as a member of one of four official racial groups — white, black, coloured and 'Asiatic' ('Indian') — with the vote reserved for whites only.

Then came the **POPULATION REGISTRATION ACT**, to reinforce the policing and administration of race classification. Henceforth a white person was officially defined as 'a person generally accepted as a white person and not in appearance obviously not white.' Race classification officials used physical appearance to determine 'race' but in 'borderline' cases hair was examined closely, a comb being pulled through it on the basis that the thicker the hair the more likely the person was to be 'non white'. In one Pretoria case, an abandoned child, Lize Venter, was classified as 'coloured' after laboratory examination of a strand of her hair.

On these foundations the massive brickwork of hundreds of Apartheid laws was erected over the ensuing years. Of the 317 Apartheid laws finally passed, the following were the key statutes:

THE MIXED MARRIAGES ACT made it a crime for any marriage to take place between a white person and a person of any other racial group.

THE IMMORALITY ACT made it a crime for any sexual act to be committed between a white person and a non-white person. To enforce this law, police were empowered to shine flashlights into parked cars, to raid premises without warrant, to remove bed linen for laboratory examination, and to make summary arrests. Between 1950 and 1985 there were more than 24,000 prosecutions under the sexual apartheid laws, and 11,614 convictions.

THE GROUP AREAS ACT proclaimed the racial zoning of South Africa. Areas were defined within which only members of specified race groups could live or occupy premises. 84% of the territory was designated for whites only, although whites made up barely 15% of the population. 2% was reserved for either 'coloureds' or 'Indians'. Taking the country as a whole, blacks, over 80% of the population, were restricted to ownership or occupation of under 14% of the land — the 'tribal homelands'.

THE BANTU EDUCATION ACT segregated all educational institutions, and insisted on different syllabuses for black schoolchildren to educate them towards lower expectations of life than whites. Emphasis was to be placed on technical rather than professional training. Introducing the law, Hendrik Verwoerd said that the new system was designed to ensure that there was no place for blacks in the white-zoned communities above menial forms of labour.

THE PASS LAWS made it compulsory for blacks to carry passport-sized booklets at all times, containing their documentary permission to be in any white area for a prescribed amount of time. Failure to do so rendered them liable to imprisonment. In 1984 it was decided as a concession that black marathon runners could run through a white area if they had a photocopy of the main page of their pass book pinned to their vests.

In spite of the many restrictions against blacks in all spheres of life there is a long tradition of black intellectuality in South Africa, fostered mainly by Fort Hare University. Originally established by British missionaries Fort Hare produced many political leaders active not only within South Africa but also in Kenya, Tanzania, Malawi, Zambia and Zimbabwe. However, the university's reputation suffered when the Afrikaner Nationalist government imposed 'Bantu Education' on all educational institutions restricted to blacks, who thereafter contemptuously referred to them as 'tribal colleges'.

THE SEPARATE AMENITIES ACT legislated for the strict segregation of all public facilities, such as parks, beaches, bus stops, swimming pools, sports grounds, theatres and cinemas. A black nursemaid could be on a 'white' beach if she was looking after children, but she could not go in the water herself except in case of emergency.

This legislation was also used in justification of a ruling by the Dutch Reformed Church that blacks could enter a 'white' church to clean it but not to pray in it.

THE RAILWAY ACT and **ROAD TRANSPORTATION ACT** legislated for trains, buses and taxis to be racially segregated, though it was permissible for a black man to drive a taxi reserved for whites.

Ambulances, in line with health services, hospitals and clinics, were all segregated. When Professor Dennis Brutus, a 'coloured' man, was wounded while trying to evade political arrest on a Johannesburg street, he lay bleeding on the sidewalk for 25 minutes because the first ambulance summoned proved to be one reserved for whites — and a second ambulance, reserved for 'coloureds', had to be sent for. Many similar cases have been reported since all health facilities were segregated under the Apartheid laws.

JOB RESERVATION laws reserved certain jobs for certain race groups. A black construction worker could hammer nails into planks with the front of the hammer, but could not use its claw to extract nails — this was deemed more refined work reserved for 'coloured' and white artisans.

THE FACTORIES ACT required the owners of every new factory to make provision for separate toilets for workers in each race group.

Ultimately there were 317 such Apartheid laws. Most were largely refinements supplementing or updating these main pillars of Apartheid, but the total also includes the 'Security' laws designed to prevent effective opposition to Apartheid — among them, the **Public Safety Act**, the **General Law Amendment Act**, the **Criminal Procedure Amendment Act**, the **Suppression of Communism Act**, the **Unlawful Organisations Act**, the **Terrorism Act**, the **Riotous Assemblies Act** and the **Internal Security Act**.

Taken together, these statutes empowered the Afrikaner Nationalist Party Government to:

Imprison anyone without trial

Banish anyone from any part of the country to another

Forbid anyone to speak in public

Forbid anyone to write for publication

Forbid anyone to travel

Forbid anyone to be in any room with more than one other person

Ban any gathering, march, meeting or demonstration

Ban any organisation

Confiscate the passport of any citizen without explanation

Enter any premises without a search warrant.

Under these statutes it was made unlawful to express or mobilise any significant opposition to Apartheid, and organisations such as the African National Congress and the Pan-Africanist Congress, the two most effective movements of black resistance to Apartheid, were outlawed.

In 1960 the Afrikaner Nationalist Party declared South Africa a republic, causing its exclusion from the Commonwealth of Nations, the countries originally part of the British Empire.

The Broederbond and the Afrikaner Nationalist Party cabinet, influenced by Hendrik Verwoerd, then began to institute territorial segregation not only on broad racial lines, but also on the basis of newly invented ethnic sub-groupings. It was no longer enough to segregate people into the categories 'white', 'black', 'coloured' and 'Indian'. Black Africans were now classified into no fewer than nine categories. (Thus the Nguni were to be fragmented into Zulus, Xhosas and others). Furthermore, each group was allocated its own 'tribal homeland' (or 'Bantustan') for the purpose of exercising some sort of vote even if its 'citizens' did not live there.

Verwoerd started his 'homelands' policy with the Transkei Territory, long set aside as a black reservation, and from this built up the blueprint for what was to be called Grand, or Total Apartheid.

His theory was an extension of the narrow interpretation of Calvinism subscribed to by the first Afrikaners. If God had determined that all species (even sub-species or types) of life were separate and distinct, then surely all differences had to be preserved and emphasised. And this means enforcing the ethnic subdivisions among blacks.

Besides, it was a convenient way to divide and rule.

The new theory was supposed to replace the older notion of *'baasskap'* (the Afrikaans word for 'boss-hood'), the dictatorship of a white minority over a black majority with the 'preponderance of control' of five million whites over all the other ethnic sub-groups.

In the special mathematics of Afrikaner Nationalism this entirely changed the moral basis of Apartheid. As expounded by Verwoerd, Apartheid had 'developed' into an idealistic system for preserving the special cultures of 'the various peoples' of South Africa.

As a result, by decision of the Broederbond as endorsed by the Afrikaner Nationalist Party Government (in most cases the same people), the map of South Africa was redrawn and the 'homelands' defined.

Parts of the designated homelands were as spotty as a Dalmatian dog.

Of the nine 'homelands' four were ultimately decreed to be 'independent' — Transkei, Ciskei, Venda and Bophuthatswana — with the rest scheduled to follow. KwaZulu, set aside for the Zulu 'nation', had so many fragments (to avoid encroaching on white farms) that on one stretch of highway under 100 miles in length, 'independence' would have meant 23 frontier posts.

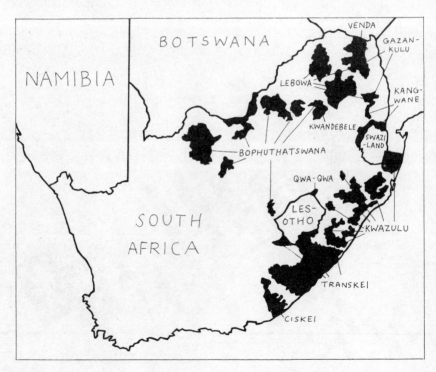

Between 1948, when it came to power, and 1977, when it reached the peak of its control over the whole South African population, the Afrikaner Nationalist Party appeared impervious to any black challenge. It even announced that the logical outcome of Grand Apartheid was that eventually there would be no black South African citizens at all — they would all be 'citizens' of one or other 'homeland', whether they wanted to be or not.

But in 1977 the whole design started to come unstuck, and it is necessary to backtrack to the beginnings of black political resistance to understand why.

As we saw earlier, black resistance had begun as soon as the first Dutch settlers arrived and encountered opposition from the Khoi and the San. Then came the territorial wars of the Afrikaners and the British against the Nguni — the Zulus in Natal and Xhosas in the Cape. And finally black people turned to political organisation to seek their rights. The first important black groups emerged in the 1880s, such as the Native Electoral Association, the African Political Organisation, and the Organisation of United Africans, led largely by Xhosas of the Eastern Cape. One of the most significant of the early leaders was Dr T Jabavu, who founded the Cape Native Convention in 1887.

Soon the movement towards independent political organisation spread elsewhere. In 1894 Mahatma Gandhi set up the Natal Indian Congress and in 1900 the Natal Native Congress was founded by John Dube, Josiah Gumede, Saul Msane, Mark Radebe and Martin Luthuli.

It soon became apparent that a nation-wide organisation was necessary to coordinate the disparate movements. In 1902 the South African Native Congress was founded in the Eastern Cape, and in 1912 the South African Native National Congress, soon to be renamed the South African National Congress, and then the African National Congress, the name by which it is still known today.

The founders of this umbrella organisation for all black resistance groups were more than a hundred delegates from all parts of South Africa, including Dube, Rubusana, Molema, Makgatho, Seme, Plaatje, Mapikela, Mangena and Msimang, with Pixley ka Seme as one of the prime movers. In part, the new organisation grew in reaction to the failure of the more conciliatory approach of Jabavu, who set up his own South African Races Congress as a body relying on the goodwill of white liberals for future progress towards civil rights for blacks.

But the African National Congress soon forged ahead to become the main movement for black rights in South Africa, and though there were to be other major movements (such as the Non-European Unity Movement, the Pan-Africanist Congress and the Black Consciousness Movement), the ANC was to prove the most durable in terms of structural organisation both internally and externally.

There were to be many divergences in the approaches of the various black groups. An early difference was in their reaction to the first Land Acts of the newly independent South African Parliament. For example, Jabavu backed the 1913 Land Act which set aside black reservations on the grounds that otherwise whites would eventually own *all* land in South Africa. The ANC split over the issue, some members supporting Dube, who had no objection to segregation in principle provided blacks got enough out of the deal, while others backed Makgatho, who completely rejected racial zoning. Makgatho carried the organisation with him on the question, and he became president of the ANC in 1917.

The first violent effect of the land segregation policy was the Bulhoek Massacre of 1921, when a community of black people refused to move from land they had occupied at Bulhoek, near Queenstown, in defiance of racial zoning. When they charged at a police patrol sent to evict them, the police opened fire and killed 163.

The ANC became more militant after Bulhoek, though its methods remained non-violent. Up until 1960, the year of the next major massacre at Sharpeville, the ANC limited its political action to passive resistance, disciplined marches, petitions to the white government, and demonstrations. Its commitment to parliamentary democracy as a principle was underlined by its symbolic use of a mace during formal debates.

When the Afrikaner Nationalist Party came to power under Malan in 1948, there was a last desperate attempt by blacks to head off the institution of full Apartheid in a series of huge demonstrations and marches.

In what was known as the Defiance Campaign, thousands ignored the curfew and pass laws and marched silently through the white cities, ending their marches at police stations where they offered themselves for arrest.

The new government responded with violence: hundreds were killed in several cities when police opened fire on the demonstrators.

Not all whites were hostile to black rights though. Many white soldiers, shocked at the election of the Malanites, declared that they hadn't fought a war in Europe against fascism only to see a fascist government installed in power when they got home. Some even formed a militant organisation, the Torch Commando, whose torch emblem was a symbol of liberty.

Pitched battles were fought between the Torch Commando and the Ossewa-Brandwag's Stormjaers, who admired Hitler and saw in their new government a resurgence of fascist principle in the face of the 'decadence of democracy'.

In 1952 the Torch Commando came near to literally frightening the Afrikaner Nationalist government out of power. In a massive demonstration in the centre of Cape Town, they tore down the iron railings and battered at the doors of Parliament itself, inside which Prime Minister Malan and his cabinet colleagues were locked in fear.

But after two speakers appealed for calm the moment passed. The marchers dispersed, never again to be a factor in South African politics. Except for a few small groups led by whites, black people were on their own.

One such group was the Liberal Party, led by author Alan Paton, which called for universal franchise for all citizens regardless of race. When multi-racial membership of political parties was made illegal the Liberal Party disbanded rather than comply.

Another was and is the Black Sash, an organisation mostly of white women committed to the cause of freedom for all. Originally called the Women's Defence of the Constitution League, it formed to oppose the Senate Act which led to the removal of voting rights for 'coloureds'. The Black Sash got its name because its first demonstrations were pickets of cabinet ministers wherever they went, the women wearing black sashes of mourning for the death of constitutional law in South Africa. Although comprised mostly of middle class white women, the Black Sash became increasingly radical under the vigorous leadership of Sheena Duncan and won lasting regard from the black community for its consistent opposition to Apartheid and for the 'advice offices' it organised in all the main cities to help black people enmeshed in the complicated regulations of the Pass Laws.

The small but militant South African Communist Party was an early and constant ally of the African National Congress, along with the Congress of Democrats and the South African Indian Congress. Its leader was a remarkable Afrikaner, Abraham Fischer, close friend of the ANC leaders and a lifelong fighter against racism.

100

Another Afrikaner who broke from the *volksideaal* to devote his life to the cause of equal rights for all was Beyers Naude, former minister of the Dutch Reformed Church of South Africa and former member of the Broederbond. As leader of the Christian Institute of South Africa he was banned in 1977 but continued his campaign as far as was practical under the banning restrictions.

The only other white group of significance at this time was the small Progressive Party, whose sole parliamentary representative for more than a decade, Helen Suzman, exposed and opposed the excesses of Apartheid single-handedly in the all-white forum. Reconstituted as the Progressive Federal Party, this became the official opposition when it supplanted the more conservative United Party, formerly led by Smuts, and increased its parliamentary representation to 27 members.

Faced with an intransigent government determined to extend Apartheid, blacks were becoming increasingly frustrated. Some members of the ANC Youth, impatient with what they regarded as the excessive caution of their elders and critical of alliances the ANC had forged with groups which included white communists, broke away under the leadership of Robert Sobukwe to form the Pan-Africanist Congress, a blacks-only organisation which immediately became more militantly aggressive than the ANC.

Support for the PAC mushroomed among angry young blacks as both the PAC and the ANC held protest gatherings to burn their pass books. It was at one such gathering on 21 March 1960 at Sharpeville, a small town near Johannesburg, that police opened fire in a volley of shots that were to echo around the world.

69 black people were shot dead and 186 were wounded. Many were shot in the back as they fled.

The shooting, which came to be known as the Sharpeville Massacre, publicised Apartheid throughout the world as nothing else had done. Up to that time the nature of Apartheid had not been widely known abroad, but overnight South Africa was recognised as a land of institutionalised racism — racism actually written into statute law — and on that one day South Africa passed into a new relationship with the rest of the international community.

Another result of Sharpeville was that South African whites passed into a new relationship with blacks. Black people previously committed to non-violent methods of resistance now

had no answers to those pressing for more militancy. After all,
they were —

not allowed to demonstate peacefully

not allowed to belong to their own organisations

not allowed to vote

not allowed to organise resistance campaigns.

They resolved to fight back.

The ANC and the PAC both formed military wings — the ANC created Umkhonto weSizwe (Spear of the Nation), and the PAC created Poqo (We Alone). Both went underground at home but set up external missions abroad.

From the beginning, the PAC's response to Sharpeville was more precipitate than that of the ANC. Wanting 'to fight and to fight NOW', the PAC hastily armed groups with whatever weapons they could find — chiefly cane-knives, axes and sticks but also some firearms, though most of these were homemade. Several cities and villages were attacked and a number of whites killed, but the campaign was easily thwarted. The police forces were better-equipped and able to draw on a wide network of paid informers in the black townships.

The ANC's Umkhonto weSizwe, under the leadership of Nelson Mandela, was more deliberate and less aggressive in its concept of armed struggle; it still wanted to give the white minority a chance to see sense and negotiate a democratic constitution. Mandela ruled that where violence was to be used at all it should be directed not against people but against property. Electricity pylons, railway lines, unstaffed military and police installations, empty barracks — any of these were appropriate targets for sabotage.

Mandela's mentor and leader of the ANC at this time, Chief Albert Luthuli of Natal, had long espoused the cause of non-violence and had been awarded the 1960 Nobel Peace Prize. But now he was deprived of his chieftainship, banned by the state and confined to his home, so Mandela had to provide leadership to channel the growing anger of the young militants of the ANC.

Mandela was born in the Transkei into the Thembu royal household of the Xhosas. He began his studies at Fort Hare, a university for black people, but was suspended from classes for political activity. Moving to Johannesburg he put himself through law school and went into partnership with his close friend Oliver Tambo. Both rose to prominent positions in the ANC Youth League.

In June 1955, Mandela was involved in organising the multi-racial Congress of the People, which was attended by delegates from all over the country. The Congress drew up the Freedom Charter. The Charter, soon adopted by the ANC as its official policy and still its most important statement of principles, begins with these words.

THE FREEDOM CHARTER

We, the people of South Africa, declare for all our country and the world to know:

That South Africa belongs to all who live in it, black and white, and that no government can justly claim authority unless it is based on the will of the people;

That our people have been robbed of their birthright to land, liberty and peace by a form of government founded on injustice and inequality;

That our country will never be prosperous or free until all our people live in brotherhood, enjoying equal rights and opportunities;

That only a democratic state, based on the will of all the people, can secure to all their birthright without distinction of colour, race, sex or belief;

And therefore we, the people of South Africa, black and white together — equals, countrymen and brothers — adopt this Freedom Charter. And we pledge ourselves to strive together, sparing neither strength nor courage, until the democratic changes here set out have been won.

THE PEOPLE SHALL GOVERN!

(The entire Freedom Charter is reproduced in an appendix.)

Following the adoption of the Freedom Charter the police arrested 156 people, including Mandela, Luthuli and Tambo, and held them pending charges for Treason, the accusation being that they planned the violent overthrow of the government. The proceedings against them went on for more than three years before all the accused were acquitted for lack of evidence.

In 1961 Mandela slipped out of the country to organise international alliances. Gaining support throughout Africa, he returned to organise internal resistance and was hunted by the police. (So successful was he in eluding them that the newspapers dubbed him the Black Pimpernel.)

But in August 1962 Mandela was arrested at a roadblock, posing as a chauffeur for a wealthy white friend. He was sentenced to five years' imprisonment for leaving the country illegally and organising strikes. But when police, aided by an informer, raided premises of Umkhonto weSizwe and found explosives, Mandela was tried again and sentenced to life imprisonment.

Shortly after Sharpeville, Mandela's friend Oliver Tambo had been sent abroad by the ANC to develop overseas missions and consolidate international support. For years after Mandela's imprisonment much of the ANC's energies went into the establishment of training camps for guerillas in several African countries in preparation for the first phases of armed struggle.

As we have seen, the initial phase ordered by Mandela was to sabotage inanimate objects and symbols of minority rule. But if the white minority stayed intransigent, attack was to be shifted to military and police personnel. And should this fail to move whites to negotiate with the black majority, a full scale civil war would be declared.

The PAC, after its initial attacks on white communities, adopted an approach more like that of the ANC. They set up training camps abroad and developed international support, but though they achieved equal recognition with the ANC in the United Nations and the Organisation of African Unity, they were unable to match the organisational scope of the ANC abroad or the scale of its financial backing.

The ANC and PAC external missions found a ready response from African countries, whose support was limited only by their capacity to help financially. It took many years to make headway in Europe, though, where they came up against a wall of ignorance about South Africa — apart from a general abhorrence of Apartheid occasioned largely by the Sharpeville Massacre — and a wall of aversion to the resort to armed struggle. There was at that time a reluctance in the West to accept the ANC argument that with legitimate politics closed to them, black people were left with no other course of action.

The ANC and PAC turned first to the West for aid and were rebuffed, but when they accepted aid from the East they were branded by South African embassy officials in Washington and London as 'communist' terrorists, although major support was also supplied by Third World countries and by European countries such as Sweden and Holland.

SOLOMON MAHLANGU
FREEDOM COLLEGE

Dutch support for the ANC was particularly resented by Afrikaner Nationalists, who felt their "mother country" should take their side. But many Dutch people argued that support for Apartheid was unthinkable, that the Apartheid version of Dutch Reformed Church theology was a perversion, and that justice — not blood ties — was the issue. Nor was it forgotten in Holland that many Afrikaner Nationalists were pro-Nazi at a time when the Luftwaffe were bombing Rotterdam and Holland was being invaded.

During their first 15 years in power the Afrikaner Nationalists, with vast funds at their disposal, won the propaganda war for the hearts and minds of Westerners hands down. They found it relatively easy to neutralize the representations of people like Tambo on the international scene, but they also had to cope with several profoundly threatening developments inside and outside South Africa which they could do little to control. After Sharpeville there was a major flight of investment capital from South Africa which emphasised that Apartheid could not be sustained indefinitely without economic and diplomatic support from the West. But the realisation of their vulnerability had already been developing for some years among the Nationalists.

114

On coming to power in 1948, Afrikaner Nationalists had believed they could now do as they wished in their reclaimed Promised Land. ('Even the trees look different'). And although India was already making Apartheid an issue in the United Nations, Western countries weren't much interested. They had other preoccupations, like the Cold War.

Yet external events, particularly in Africa, began to challenge the Afrikaner Nationalists' long-held view of that continent as one easily controllable by white minorities. During and after World War Two, former colonial possessions had begun their moves towards independence in a process whose outcome was decided ultimately by simple demographic arithmetic. Even where the ruling white minorities had bitterly resisted black majority rule, the inevitable march of these states to independence went on.

Italy lost Libya and Somalia

France lost Algeria and Tunisia

Spain lost Morocco and parts of the Sahara

Belgium lost Zaire

Portugal lost Angola and Mozambique

Britain lost Kenya, Nigeria, Ghana, Tanzania, Uganda, Zambia and Malawi.

In 1960, the British Prime Minister Harold Macmillan had warned white South Africa of the strength of African nationalism. In a speech to Parliament in Cape Town he warned of the 'Winds of Change' sweeping Africa. The implication was clear — they were heading south, straight for Cape Town.

Another external pressure was the question of Namibia.

After Premier Louis Botha had captured 'South West Africa' from the Germans in World War 1, the grateful Allies had mandated the area to South Africa through the League of Nations, to act as a guardian and tutor for the territory's independence.

But from the beginning the territory was treated by South Africa virtually as a fifth province, and there were moves to incorporate it formally as part of the Union of South Africa. And when the Afrikaner Nationalist Party took power in 1948, the new administration moved quickly to establish its claim by having it return representatives to the South African Parliament.

The two major Namibian liberation groups, the South West African People's Organisation (SWAPO) and the South West African National Union (SWANU), succeeded in making the issue of their independence an international one. (In recent years SWAPO has gained the ascendancy and is recognised as the liberation movement most representative of the people of the territory).

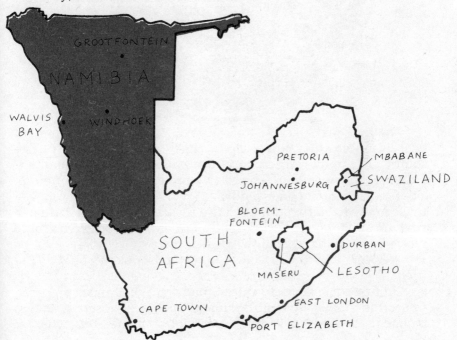

The Namibia question became a thorn in the flesh of the Afrikaner Nationalists, but in spite of world-wide condemnation they refused to quit the territory, and installed an army there to enforce their rule. SWAPO responded by forming its own army, and guerrilla war began in 1966.

International reaction to Sharpeville, pressure from abroad over Namibia, the Winds of Change blowing independence southward through Africa, and the exclusion from the Commonwealth of the new South African Republic — not to mention an assassination attempt on Hendrik Verwoerd by a white farmer — caused the Broederbond to steer the Afrikaner National Party in a new direction. They decided that Apartheid must be given a more moral basis in the eyes of the world.

Verwoerd believed that his 'homelands' policy would do the trick.

At first some governments abroad were generously prepared to see the 'homelands' or 'Bantustan' policy as a sort of 'down payment' towards a genuine partition scheme. But when it became clear that the white minority under such 'partition' would take most of the best land and leave the black majority the little that remained, the international community rejected the idea as comprehensively as black South Africans themselves did. No foreign country was to recognise the 'independence' of any of the Bantustans, and by 1986 the only 'embassies' there were South African ones. (South Africa thus became the first country in history to establish an embassy on its own soil.)

In September 1966, Hendrik Verwoerd was stabbed to death at his desk in the debating chamber of the South African Parliament by a (white) parliamentary messenger, and Balthazar Johannes Vorster became Prime Minister.

Vorster, who had been imprisoned by Smuts during World War 2 as a leader of the pro-Nazi Ossewa-Brandwag, soon made an executive decision which isolated South Africa on yet another front. He banned the proposed tour of an England cricket team to South Africa because one of the England players, Basil D'Oliveira, was 'coloured'. The ban on D'Oliveira, who was born in South Africa but had gone to England because South African law prevented him playing for his own country, touched off a worldwide boycott of South African sports teams.

Three other events further increased South Africa's isolation from the international community:

● The Soweto riots in 1976

● The Biko killing in 1977

● Widespread violence throughout South Africa in 1985 and 1986.

The Soweto riots began when police opened fire on black schoolchildren in the township of Soweto, near Johannesburg. (The name 'Soweto' is an abbreviation of South Western Townships). The children resented having to be educated through the medium of the Afrikaans language, which many blacks regard as 'the language of the oppressor'. They fought back for days against police guns and tear gas with nothing more than sticks, stones, and occasional hastily-fashioned petrol bombs. More than 600 of the children were killed in violence that spread from Soweto to other black townships throughout the country.

Steve Biko was the leading spirit in the formation of the Black Consciousness Movement which awakened blacks to a new sensitivity to their oppression. Biko aimed to 'rid the colonised of their slave mentality', to inculcate black pride and to make 'blackness, the reason for our oppression, the symbol of our liberation'. He also urged unity between the ANC and PAC, a development long feared by the Afrikaner Nationalist government. He was imprisoned without trial for the fourth time in August 1977, and on September 12 he died in Security Police custody of brain damage caused by several blows to the head.

His death caused a worldwide outcry and led to an increase in diplomatic and economic pressure against the Apartheid government.

He was one of more than 100 activists to die violently while in Security Police custody.

Since August 1984, following the introduction of a new constitution in South Africa which allowed separate representation of a limited nature to 'coloured' and 'Indian' South Africans but excluded all African blacks, black township after black township exploded into violence, making large areas of the country virtually ungovernable. The response of the Afrikaner Nationalist Party was to declare a State of Emergency and to arrest thousands of demonstrators in various parts of the country. The violence, and the State of Emergency, caused the biggest withdrawal yet of foreign investment capital, and after a sharp decline in its currency, South Africa announced its first-ever default on overseas bank loan repayments — a move which further increased international pressure.

In 1978 Vorster resigned the Premiership after aides disclosed large scale misuse of public funds by certain officials in the propaganda campaign led by Minister C.P. Mulder, Vorster's heir-apparent to the Premiership. This became known as the 'Muldergate' scandal. Vorster was succeeded to the Premiership by Pieter W. Botha, an excitable man with a colourful past.

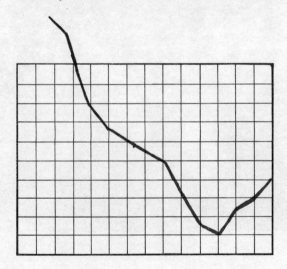

Pieter Botha was born in the Orange Free State in 1916. In 1936 he became a party organiser for the Afrikaner Nationalist Party, playing a leading role in the party's campaign to prevent Jewish refugees and other Onnasionale elemente (un-national elements) being allowed into South Africa. During World War 2, and in the period up to the party's 1948 election victory, Botha became noted as leader of gangs of Stormjaers (party toughs) who broke up meetings of the Smuts party and harassed speakers favourable to the Allied cause. Before being appointed to head the military ministry, Botha was Minister of Coloured Affairs, and as such played a leading role in ordering the removal of an entire community of 'coloured' people from an area of Cape Town, District Six, where they and their families had lived for hundreds of years. This removal was in line with the Group Areas Act, passed in order to keep the cities for white residents only. The District Six 'coloured' community were moved miles beyond the city to a bleak area called the Cape Flats.

Even before Botha took over as Prime Minister, the Afrikaner Nationalist Party cabinet and Broederbond had decided that the propaganda war abroad was going less well than it had, and that a better image should be sought.

The snag was that while they wanted to appear more reasonable to people overseas, they feared losing support from right-wing conservatives back home if they made any concessions. The extreme right wing had already broken away to form the Herstigte Nasionale Party, calling for a return to undiluted Baasskap (boss-hood) and 'Pure' Apartheid.

The result, for a brief period, was the 'multinational' policy, the brainchild of minister and sometime Broederbond chief Piet Koornhof. This meant that under certain conditions, and with the appropriate permission, blacks would be allowed to play sport with whites in their various capacities as members of different 'nations' rather than of different *races* — which meant the Afrikaner Nationalists could reassure their right-wing supporters that they were not allowing multi-racial sport, only multi-national sport.

The same principle was applied in certain hotels and restaurants, and even on some beaches, depending on whether the hotel or restaurant applied for and was given 'international status'. (It was not explained how a beach could apply for international status).

An offshoot of the 'Bantustan' or 'Homelands' policy was the establishment of casino resorts like Sun City in Bophutatswana, an oasis of opulence in the midst of grinding black poverty — where rich whites could gamble, watch sex shows, date black girls and read magazines like Playboy — all illegal activities across the 'border' in 'white' South Africa.

The Afrikaner Nationalist government felt that by these devices it could keep its electoral pledges to the party faithful to segregate the races, while at the same time telling the world that segregation on the basis of race was being phased out.

At the United Nations, Foreign Minister 'Pik' Botha (no relation of P.W. Botha) spoke of South Africa turning away from racial discrimination. And Piet Koornhof told the National Press Club in Washington that 'Apartheid is dead!'

The trick, of course, was to discriminate against blacks not as blacks, but as 'foreign' citizens of homeland states!!

The same thing had happened in previous examples of statutory segregation, as in Alabama and Mississippi before the Civil Rights movement. In the last throes of segregation the segregationists began to talk in code. They no longer spoke of 'keeping niggers in their place.' They referred instead to 'states' rights'. Instead of 'white superiority', they referred to 'maintaining standards'.

South Africa's version of code language permutes terms like 'multi-nationalism', 'separate development', 'parallel development', 'cooperative co-existence' and 'power-sharing'. All are euphemisms intended to stave off full equality.

Even the terms used to denote black people in South Africa have continuously mutated.

At first blacks were called Kaffirs (niggers). Then they were called Naturelle (natives). Then they were called Bantoe (Bantu). Then they were called Africans. Now the word is blacks.

When P.W. Botha took over as Prime Minister in 1978, he said that 'reform' was on the way, that white South Africans must 'adapt or die,' and that he would lead them in such reform.

He said he would consider removing the Immorality Act, the law forbidding inter-racial marriage or sexual relations, and five years later he did so. (The Immorality Act was a white obsession rather than a black concern. To most blacks the Immorality Act was the least of their Apartheid problems.)

He also allowed greater latitude in certain 'mixed' amenities, and in the formation of legal black trade unions and in black rights to temporary tenure in white zones.

These 'reforms' were the consequence not only of internal militancy among blacks but also because of external pressures on the economy. Divestment moves in America and Europe struck real fear into the hearts of the Afrikaner Nationalists, who saw them as the forerunners of economic sanctions, which they knew would further shorten the lifespan of Apartheid.

For years the main thrust of their propaganda abroad was aimed at heading off such sanctions, and an elaborate mythology had been created at vast expense, partly through the 'Muldergate' disinformation projects, to plant certain reasonable sounding but false ideas firmly in the minds of Western decision-makers.

Ideas such as:

Black South Africans were against sanctions, as these would 'hurt them the most'

(**Wrong**. All credible black leaders urged sanctions, and polls showed a large black majority in favour.)

Black people in South Africa were economically better off than blacks anywhere else in Africa.

(**Wrong**. Per capita Gross National Product figures put them 13th in Africa, behind Kenya, Gabon, Nigeria, Ghana, Algeria, Libya, Tunisia, Niger, Ivory Coast, Botswana and Zimbabwe.)

Zulus, the 'biggest tribe in South Africa', favoured limited power-sharing.

(**Wrong**. There are at least as many Xhosa as Zulus, and besides all Nguni call for full democracy.)

The West is completely dependent on South Africa for strategic minerals.

(**Wrong**. A comprehensive two-year U.S. Senate study established that alternative sources could be found.)

If sanctions were applied, the Afrikaner Nationalist government could expel more than a million foreign black workers.

(**Wrong**. More than 940,000 of the workers referred to were 'homelands citizens' and therefore 'foreign' only in the eyes of the South African Government itself.)

Black South Africans were divided into mutually-hostile tribes with separate and divergent political aspirations.

(**Wrong**. Tribalism wasn't a major factor in black politics in South Africa, and the call for unity in liberation had general support.)

Black liberation movements were communist-dominated and hostile to long-term Western interests.

(**Wrong**. Their leaders were non-communist campaigners for orthodox democracy and for non-aligned status internationally.)

The 'Cape Sea Route' could be lost to the West if blacks governed South Africa.

(**Wrong**. The 'Cape Sea Route' had not existed since the days of sailing ships with limited supply capacity.)

White-ruled South Africa constituted a 'bastion of the West' against communism.

(**Wrong**. White-ruled South Africa constituted a continuing embarrassment to the West in its relations with the Third World.)

Reforms short of full democracy could obviate inter-racial conflict.

(**Wrong**. Nothing short of one person — one vote could meet black aspirations.)

One of the 'reforms' announced by Prime Minister Botha was a change of constitution making him President and setting up a tricameral Parliament in which 'coloureds' and 'Indians' would have representation. (It stacked the cards against the two smaller groups by building in a white majority vote.)

This failed to please the majority of the 'Coloureds' and 'Indians', most of whom boycotted the elections. Nor did it impress the world. And it enraged the black majority who were specifically excluded from any central representation.

In fact, the new constitution triggered off angry demonstra-

JACKSON

tions throughout South Africa which in turn made the Apartheid issue prominent in domestic American politics. During 1984 and 1985 campaigns in America for divestment and sanctions against South Africa developed broad support, not least among the 35 million black Americans. Their awareness was further raised when the presidential candidate, Rev. Jesse Jackson, made Apartheid an election issue in the United States, and a South African moderate, Bishop Desmond Tutu, found that mass media platforms were made available to him when he was awarded the Nobel Peace Prize.

A further factor was the collapse of the Reagan Administration's 'Constructive Engagement' policy.

The notion of 'Constructive Engagement' was based on three false assumptions:

US hostility would drive the Afrikaner Nationalists further into the 'laager' and increase the severity of their repressive system.

The best way to eliminate Apartheid would be by reasoning with them as allies.

That significant reforms would result and Namibia would be freed.

The policy was tried for seven years but it didn't work. On the contrary, the Afrikaner Nationalists interpreted 'Constructive Engagement' as tacit support for their supremacy in southern Africa. As a result they launched invasions or raids into Mozambique, Angola, Lesotho, Botswana and even the Seychelles Islands, in attempts to set up regimes favourable to themselves. They also escalated the war in Namibia, and within the first four years of 'Constructive Engagement' killed more blacks in southern Africa than previous administrations had done in the preceding quarter-century.

By mid-1986 even the Reagan administration was beginning to cool to the Afrikaner Nationalists. Congress and Senate insisted on a tougher line against Apartheid, including economic sanctions. Similar pressures began to build up in the European Economic Community and the Commonwealth.

It was long recognised that the U.S.A. and Britain held the key to the strongest economic sanctions, because they had the largest investment and trade interests in South Africa, and both had repeatedly used their power of veto in the United Nations Security Council to block the international call for comprehensive mandatory sanctions.

But in 1986 Britain and the United States began to perceive the danger to their own national interests of close involvement with the Afrikaner Nationalist administration in South Africa, and Pretoria began to feel the beginnings of a chill from London and Washington.

So 1986 marked the first major confluence of external as well as internal challenges to Apartheid, with economic and diplomatic threats from abroad and social and political turmoil in all the major cities in South Africa.

Debate raged within the ruling circle of the Afrikaner Nationalist Party as to how to respond. Dr Andries Treurnicht had broken away to form the Conservative Party as a home for disaffected right-wing extremists, for whom any concession was a surrender of pure Apartheid. On the other hand, the Progressive Federal Party in parliamentary opposition declared the Botha 'reforms' inadequate, and the leader of the party, Dr Van Zyl Slabbert, resigned to seek extra-parliamentary alliances against the Botha regime.

South Africa's business community, alarmed at the deterioration of the economy resulting from governmental intransigence, demanded more significant reforms and real negotiations with credible black leaders. But most of the reformists in the white community refused to face the fact that 'power-sharing' was not a viable option if it fell short of one person — one vote, the minimum demand of the black majority.

As had happened in Kenya, Rhodesia and other white minority-ruled countries on the eve of independence, whites began to search for evasions of democracy. There was talk of 'confederation', of 'A voting rolls' and 'B voting rolls', of 'qualified franchise', and even of territorial partition — some of which might have worked as temporary compromises a quarter of a century ago, but the hands of the political clock had moved far beyond these notions in South Africa and no credible black leader could be expected to take them seriously.

By mid 1986 the Afrikaner Nationalists were drifting further and further away from reality. Although they talked of scrapping the Group Areas Act, the pass laws, and other hated elements of the Apartheid package, they failed to see that even if 316 of the 317 Apartheid laws were abolished there would be no peace if the single surviving law was the one which kept universal franchise from the black majority.

And there was no acknowledgement among whites that the only Apartheid law that needed to be scrapped was that same franchise law; that with full democracy, blacks would soon remove the rest.

'So it's democracy or nothing?'

Right.

'One person — one vote?'

There's no other kind of democracy.

'What can I do to help the cause of democracy in South Africa?'

Everyone, everywhere, can do something. Every action, every gesture, helps — whether it is writing to your Member of Parliament or representative in Congress to urge international pressure or taking part in boycotts or demonstrations. Robert Kennedy, visiting South Africa in 1966, said:

'Each time you stand up for an ideal, or act to improve the lot of others, you send forth a tiny ripple of hope, and crossing each other from a million sources of energy these ripples build a current that can sweep down the mightiest walls of oppression.'

Apartheid is dying from revolt within and revulsion without.

Millions of ordinary people all over the world are putting pressure on their governments to oppose Apartheid meaningfully and to apply sanctions that bite. Black South Africans have reached the end of their tether and are fighting Apartheid to the death.

So that's how it all began; that's how it all developed. And that, until the last racial law is removed in South Africa, is **APARTHEID.**

'But why are the white minority so obstinate?'

There's a saying: He who mounts the tiger fears to dismount.

'So how would you sum up the future of Apartheid?

Apartheid has no future.

'How would you sum up Apartheid itself?'

Group insanity which has emerged from centuries of prejudice, hatred and fear, culminating in suicidal folly — that's Apartheid.

The world's worst example of legalised racism — that's Apartheid.

A direct descendant of Hitler's Nuremburg laws against the Jews — that's Apartheid.

A relic of the era of slavery — that's Apartheid.

The statutory codification of all the worst prejudices known to humanity — that's Apartheid.

A legacy of insult, persecution, discrimination, suffering and death — that's Apartheid.

And finally, the aberration that has imperilled a country which had everything going for it. The country with

No Winters
No Hurricanes
No Tornadoes
No Blizzards
No Earthquakes . . .

Remember?

The system that sullied Paradise — that's Apartheid.

The Freedom Charter

We, the people of South Africa, declare for all our country and the world to know:

That South Africa belongs to all who live in it, black and white, and that no government can justly claim authority unless it is based on the will of the people;

That our people have been robbed of their birthright to land, liberty and peace by a form of government founded on injustice and inequality;

That our country will never be prosperous or free until all our people live in brotherhood, enjoying equal rights and opportunities;

That only a democratic state, based on the will of all the people, can secure to all their birthright without distinction of colour, race, sex or belief;

And therefore we, the people of South Africa, black and white together — equals, countrymen and brothers — adopt this Freedom Charter. And we pledge ourselves to strive together, sparing neither strength nor courage, until the democratic changes here set out have been won.

THE PEOPLE SHALL GOVERN!

Every man and women shall have the right to vote for and to stand as a candidate for all bodies which make laws;

All people shall be entitled to take part in the administration of the country: The right of the people shall be the same, regardless of race, colour or sex;

All bodies of minority rule, advisory boards, councils and authorities shall be replaced by democratic organs of self government.

ALL NATIONAL GROUPS SHALL HAVE EQUAL RIGHTS!

There shall be equal status in the bodies of state, in the courts and in the schools for all national groups and races;

All people shall have equal right to use their own languages, and to develop their own folk culture and customs;

All national groups shall be protected by law against insults to their race and national pride;

The preaching and practice of national race or colour discrimination and contempt shall be a punishable crime;

All apartheid laws and practices shall be set aside.

THE PEOPLE SHALL SHARE IN THE COUNTRY'S WEALTH!

The national wealth of our country, the heritage of all South Africans, shall be restored to the people;

The mineral wealth beneath the soil, the Banks and monopoly industry shall be transferred to the ownership of the people as a whole;

All other industry and trade shall be controlled to assist the well-being of the people;

All people shall have equal rights to trade where they choose to manufacture and to enter all trades, crafts and professions.

THE LAND SHALL BE SHARED AMONG THOSE WHO WORK IT!

Restrictions of land ownership on a racial basis shall be ended, and all the land redivided amongst those who work it, to banish famine and land hunger;

The state shall help the peasants with implements, seed, tractors and dams to save the soil and assist the tillers;

Freedom of movement shall be guaranteed to all who work on the land;

All shall have the right to occupy land wherever they choose;

People shall not be robbed of their cattle, and forced labour and farm prisons shall be abolished.

ALL SHALL BE EQUAL BEFORE THE LAW!

No one shall be imprisoned, deported or restricted without a fair trial;

No one shall be condemned by the order of any Government official;

The courts shall be representative of all the people;

Imprisonment shall be only for serious crimes against the people, and shall aim at re-education, not vengeance;

The police force and army shall be open to all on an equal basis and shall be the helpers and protectors of the people;

All laws which discriminate on grounds of race, colour or belief shall be repealed.

ALL SHALL ENJOY EQUAL HUMAN RIGHTS!

The law shall guarantee to all their right to speak, to organise, to meet together, to publish, to preach, to worship and to educate their children;

The privacy of the house from police raids shall be protected by law;

All shall be free to travel without restriction from country-side to town, from province to province, and from South Africa abroad;

Pass Laws, permits and all other laws restricting these freedoms shall be abolished.

THERE SHALL BE WORK AND SECURITY!

All who work shall be free to form trade unions, to elect their officers and to make wage agreements with their employers;

The state shall recognise the right and duty of all to work, and to draw full unemployment benefits;

Men and women of all races shall receive equal pay for equal work;

There shall be a forty-hour working week, a national minimum wage, paid annual leave, and sick leave for all workers, and maternity leave on full pay for all working mothers;

Miners, domestic workers, farm workers and civil servants shall have the same rights as all others who work;

Child labour, compound labour, the tot system and contract labour shall be abolished.

THE DOORS OF LEARNING AND OF CULTURE SHALL BE OPENED!

The government shall discover, develop and encourage national talent for the enhancement of our cultural-life;

All the cultural treasures of mankind shall be open to all by free exchange of books, ideas and contact with other lands;

The aim of education shall be to teach the youth to love their people and their culture, to honour human brotherhood, liberty and peace.

Education shall be free, compulsory, universal and equal for all children;

Higher education and technical training shall be opened to all by means of state allowances and scholarships awarded on the basis of merit.

Adult illiteracy shall be ended by a mass state education plan;

Teachers shall have all the rights of other citizens;

The colour bar in cultural life, in sport and in education shall be abolished.

THERE SHALL BE HOUSES, SECURITY AND COMFORT!

All people shall have the right to live where they choose, to be decently housed, and to bring up their families in comfort and security;

Unused housing space to be made available to the people;

Rent and prices shall be lowered, food plentiful and no one shall go hungry;

A preventive health scheme shall be run by the state;

Free medical care and hospitalisation shall be provided for all, with special care for mothers and young children;

Slums shall be demolished, and new suburbs built where all have transport, roads, lighting, playing fields, creches and social centres;

The aged, the orphans, the disabled and the sick shall be cared for by the state;

Rest, leisure and recreation shall be the right of all;

Fenced locations and ghettoes shall be abolished, and laws which break up families shall be repealed

THERE SHALL BE PEACE AND FRIENDSHIP!

South Africa shall be a fully independent state, which respects the rights and sovereignty of all nations;

South Africa shall strive to maintain world peace and the settlement of all international disputes by negotiation — not war;

Peace and Friendship amongst all our people shall be secured by upholding the equal rights, opportunities and status of all;

The people of the protectorates — Basutoland, Bechuanaland and Swaziland — shall be free to decide for themselves their own future;

The right of all the peoples of Africa to independence and self-government shall be recognised, and shall be the basis of close co-operation.

Let all who love their people and their country now say, as we say here:

THESE FREEDOMS WE WILL FIGHT FOR, SIDE BY SIDE, THROUGHOUT OUR LIVES, UNTIL WE HAVE WON OUR LIBERTY.

Going further

A New History of Southern Africa, by Neil Parsons
(Macmillan, 1982) is a readable and well-illustrated textbook
that covers the whole region and several millennia up to the
1960s.

The classic account of the origins and development of the
ANC up to 1965 is **South Africa: The Search for a Birthright**
(IDAF, reprinted 1985). For Nelson Mandela's life and work,
see **The Struggle is my Life** *(IDAF, 1986)*, a collection of his
speeches, essays and statements, and Mary Benson's
biography, **Nelson Mandela** *(Penguin, 1985)*. Winnie
Mandela's autobiography, **Part of my Soul** *(Penguin, 1986)*, is
highly recommended.

For detailed and comprehensive analyses of life under
Apartheid in South Africa today see **The Apartheid
Handbook**, by Roger Omond *(Penguin, Harmondsworth,
1985)*, and **Apartheid: The Facts** *(IDAF — the international
Defence and Aid Fund for South Africa, 1983)*.

For Their Triumphs and Their Tears *(IDAF, 1985)* focuses on
the oppression of black women in South Africa. **Crippling a
Nation** *(IDAF, 1984)* is a damning indictment of how
Apartheid destroys the health of black people.

Three important books on South Africa's relations with the
rest of the world are **Race, Propaganda and South Africa**, by
John Laurence *(Gollancz, 1979)* **South Africa at War**, by
Richard Leonard *(Lawrence Hill, Westport, Connecticut, USA,
1983)*, and **Sanctions against South Africa — Exploding the
Myths**, by Barbara Rogers & Brian Bolton *(Manchester Free
Press, Manchester, 1981)*.

Two books by the present author are an autobiography,
Asking for Trouble *(Gollancz, 1980)* and a biography of Steve
Biko, **Biko** *(Penguin, 1978)*.

(Place of publication is London unless otherwise stated.)